MOTORCYCLE RACING

The Fast Track

Superbike

JIM MEZZANOTTE

GARETH**STEVENS**
GS
PUBLISHING
A Member of the WRC Media Family of Companies

Please visit our web site at: www.garethstevens.com
For a free color catalog describing Gareth Stevens Publishing's
list of high-quality books and multimedia programs, call
1-800-542-2595 (USA) or 1-800-387-3178 (Canada).
Gareth Stevens Publishing's fax: (414) 332-3567.

Library of Congress Cataloging-in-Publication Data

Mezzanotte, Jim.
    Superbike / by Jim Mezzanotte.
        p. cm. — (Motorcycle racing: The fast track)
    Includes bibliographical references and index.
    ISBN 0-8368-6424-7 (lib. bdg.)
    ISBN 0-8368-6573-1 (softcover)
        1. Motorcycle racing—Juvenile literature. 2. Superbikes—
    Juvenile literature. I. Title.
    GV1060.M49   2006
    796.7'5—dc22   2005027216

This edition first published in 2006 by
Gareth Stevens Publishing
A Member of the WRC Media Family of Companies
330 West Olive Street, Suite 100
Milwaukee, WI 53212 USA

This edition copyright © 2006 by Gareth Stevens, Inc.

Editor: Leifa Butrick
Cover design and layout: Dave Kowalski
Art direction: Tammy West
Picture research: Diane Laska-Swanke

Technical Advisor: Kerry Graeber

Photo credits: Cover, pp. 5, 7, 17, 21 © Brian J. Nelson; pp. 9, 11, 13, 15,
19 © Mike Doran/D&W Images

Printed in the United States of America

1 2 3 4 5 6 7 8 9 10 09 08 07 06

CONTENTS

Cover: Superbikes travel at very
high speeds, even in turns!

The World of Superbikes

Have you ever wanted to race a motorcycle? Maybe you have seen people zoom down the road on their bikes. Of course, they do not race. Racing on regular roads is illegal — and dangerous. But you could race on a track! In road racing, riders speed around tracks that are similar to regular roads. The tracks have straightaways and twisting turns.

Superbike racing is a kind of road racing. It began in the 1970s. Superbikes are fast racing bikes. They are similar to **street bikes**.

At first, superbike racing only took place in the United States. Today, it is popular around the world. It is full of high-speed action!

Road racing tracks are similar to regular roads. Riders speed through tight turns.

Superbike Races

Top **pros** compete in the U.S. championship. They earn points in each race. The rider with the most points becomes champ. AMA Pro Racing sets the rules. It is part of the American Motorcyclist Association, or AMA. Pros also race bikes that are similar to superbikes, such as supersport bikes. There is a world superbike championship, too.

Riders have to **qualify** to race. They have to be able to speed around the track. Only riders with fast times get to race. Before they start, they line up in rows on the **grid**. The fastest riders are in front. The fastest one of all has the **pole position**.

Most U.S. races are about 60 miles (100 kilometers) long. One race, the Daytona 200, is 200 miles (322 km) long.

A race begins. Riders in front often have the best chance of winning.

7

Power and Speed

Superbikes are street bikes that are **modified** for racing. They have no headlights or other things needed for street riding. They weigh less than street bikes.

Engines are modified, too. These engines are small, but they produce a lot of **horsepower**. A superbike engine has more power than some car engines!

The bikes also have lightweight fairings. A fairing covers a bike in the front and on the sides. It creates a smooth shape that cuts through the air. Fairings help the bikes go fast. Superbikes can travel more than 180 miles (290 km) per hour! The bikes have large brakes, for slowing down quickly.

Road racing bikes are light but powerful.
Fairings help them reach high speeds.

Racing Rubber

Tires are important in superbike racing. Riders speed through many twisting turns. They need tires with good **traction** on the pavement.

Superbikes use special tires, called slicks. The slicks do not have grooved **treads** like most tires. Instead, they are smooth. Slicks have a lot of rubber touching the ground. The rubber is very soft, and it wears out quickly. A normal tire lasts for several years. Slicks usually last for one race!

Slicks only work well if they are hot. They need to be hotter than boiling water! If they are too cold, they could break apart. Teams often warm the tires before a race.

A rider leans into a tight turn. The bike's slicks grip the track.

A Team Effort

In road racing, riders get help from other people. Most top pros are part of factory teams. They race for companies that make motorcycles. There are teams from Honda, Suzuki, Yamaha, Kawasaki, and Ducati. Success in racing can help them sell more bikes!

Before a race, big trucks arrive at the track. The trucks carry factory teams. Team members make sure every bike is ready to race. They fix the bikes if they break. They do whatever it takes to help their riders win.

Companies often use road racing to test new ideas. They keep improving their bikes, so the bikes will be faster on the track.

These team members are hard at work. They will make sure this bike is in top shape.

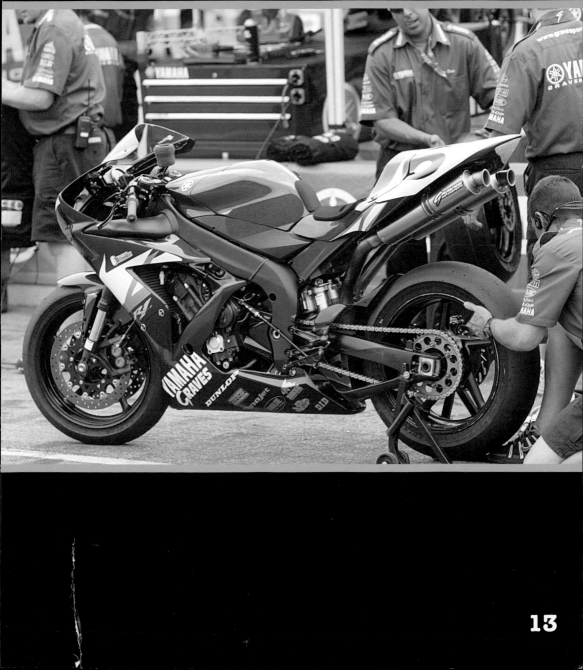

Super Skills

Racing a superbike takes skill. Pros first race as **amateurs**. They spend a lot of time learning to race. They get a special license to race as pros.

Riders need strength and balance. In turns, they lean close to the ground. Their knees may touch the pavement. They take the fastest line, or path, through each turn. Pro racers steer their bikes exactly where they need to go.

During a race, everything happens quickly. Riders are always twisting the **throttle,** shifting gears, and using the brakes. They race close together at high speeds. They look for any chance to pass, but one small mistake could mean disaster!

In turns, riders put their weight to one side. They look like they might fall off!

Staying Safe

Riders can get injured in road racing. Safety is important. Riders wear helmets to protect the head and face. They wear thick leather suits, called leathers. They also wear **pucks** on their knees. Pucks are made of smooth plastic. When riders lean into turns, the pucks slide on the pavement. Riders wear gloves and boots, too. They wear padding and tough **body armor**.

Race officials help with safety. If a rider crashes, they wave a yellow flag. Riders cannot pass when this flag is out. Officials may even wave a red flag, stopping a race. If they see a rider's bike leaking oil, they wave a black flag. That rider must leave the track.

An AMA official waves a red flag. Riders must slow down and stop their bikes.

BEGIN 50 M.P.H. PIT LANE SPEED

Superbike Stars

Mathew Mladin is a top superbike pro. He has been the AMA superbike champ five times. No other rider has been a champ this many times! He has won many big races, including the Daytona 200. Mladin is from Australia. He first raced superbikes there.

Miguel Duhamel is a top pro, too. He is the first person from Canada to be an AMA superbike champ. He has won many races.

Ben and Eric Bostrom are brothers. They both race superbikes! Ben was an AMA champ. He now competes in world superbike races. Eric is still trying to become the U.S. superbike champ. They both began riding at an early age.

Mathew Mladin speeds through a turn.
You can see the puck on his knee.

Let's Race!

It's time to race. You are on the grid, surrounded by other riders. You watch for the green light. Finally, it flashes. Rear tires spin and engines scream. The race has begun!

At the first turn, you brake hard and lean to the ground. You speed through more turns, leaning right and left. Other riders are inches from your bike. You see an opening and pass. On the straightaway, you twist the throttle and shift gears. You crouch down to cut through the air.

You hit the next turn in seconds. Coming out of the turn, you twist the throttle again. The leaders are up ahead. Will you get your chance to pass them?

In road racing, riders are often close together. It can be hard to pass!

GLOSSARY

amateurs: in sports, people who compete for fun and not to make a living.

body armor: plastic shields that protect a rider's body.

grid: in racing, the starting lineup on a track. A grid has many rows of riders, with several riders in each row. Their place in the grid depends on how well they qualify.

horsepower: the amount of power an engine produces, based on how much work one horse can do.

modified: changed in some way.

pole position: the spot at the very front of the starting grid.

pros: short for professionals. In sports, people who are very good at a sport and earn money competing in it.

pucks: in superbike racing, smooth plastic pieces that cover a rider's knees.

qualify: in racing, to earn a spot in the main race.

street bikes: motorcycles that people can ride on regular roads.

throttle: the part of a motorcycle that controls how much gas goes to the engine. Riders work the throttle by twisting one of the bike's handlebar grips.

traction: the ability of something to grip a surface.

treads: the parts of tires that touch the ground.

FURTHER INFORMATION

Books

Motorcycles. Race Car Legends (series). Jeff Savage (Chelsea House)

Superbike Racing. Motorcycles (series). Ed Youngblood (Capstone Press)

Superbikes. Designed for Success (series). Ian Graham (Heinemann)

The World's Fastest Superbikes. Built for Speed (series). Terri Sievert (Capstone Press)

Videos

RoadRace (Customflix)

World Superbike Review 2004 (Kultur)

Web Sites

www.amasuperbike.com
This web site is the official site for AMA superbike racing. It has information about races and also has photos.

www.benbostrom.com
At this web site, you can learn more about Ben Bostrom.

www.hondaredriders.com/roadracing/raceresults.asp?bhcp=1 #Series1
This web page is part of the Honda racing team's web site. You can see pictures of Miguel Duhamel competing in many races.

www.motodemons.com/IsSuper.htm
Visit this site to see pictures from a superbike race at Laguna Seca Raceway, in California.

INDEX